DRINKING
BORDEAUX

Château la Dame Blanche. *One of the most graceful mansions in the Medoc, now owned by the Cruse family. It is the traditional home of the White Lady 'La Dame de Blanquefort' whose ghost may still be seen on autumn mornings bringing prosperity to her vineyards.*

The 'Drinking for Pleasure' Series

DRINKING BORDEAUX

WRITTEN & WITH ILLUSTRATIONS BY

YOUNGMAN CARTER

HAMISH HAMILTON

LONDON

First published in Great Britain, 1966
by Hamish Hamilton Ltd
90 Great Russell Street London WC1
Copyright © 1966 by P. & M. Youngman Carter Ltd.

Printed in Great Britain by
W. & J. Mackay & Co Ltd, Chatham, Kent

CONTENTS

ILLUSTRATIONS

MAPS

'Drink no longer water, but use a little wine
for thy stomach's sake.'

I. TIMOTHY. V. 23

'For wine inspires us and fires us with courage,
love and joy.'

JOHN GAY

'I often wonder what the Vintners buy
One half so precious as the goods they sell.'

FITZGERALD

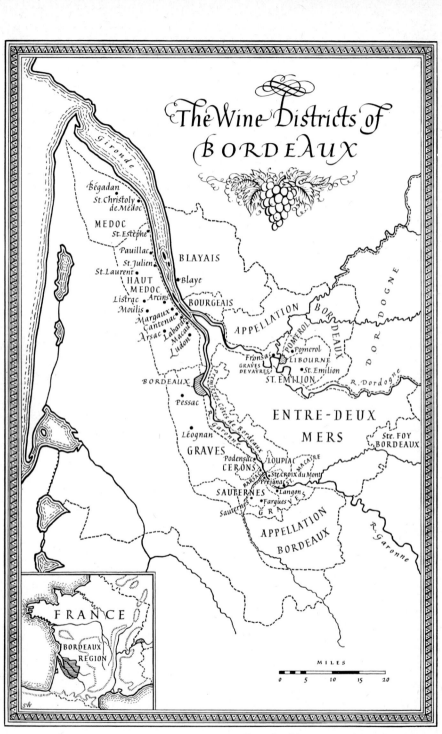

The Wine Districts of BORDEAUX

Reproduced by courtesy of Harveys of Bristol

Of Wines in General

THE difference between a glass of red wine and a vintage claret, is either non-existent or absolute, according to individual taste.

The same may be said of the merits of a strip-cartoon and a sketch by Augustus John: both can be described as drawings and both give pleasure.

Again, to encounter a Chopin étude played by an amateur may be tolerable, even pleasant, but to hear the same work from the hands of Ashkenazy is to listen to a miracle. Yet both come under the general heading of music and a total stranger to the subject could be forgiven for being enraptured by the first version. Only comparison could show him the difference and open his ears to a new world.

With wine the qualities, subtleties and variations are as infinite as with any other gift from the Almighty and only comparison of the elementary with the better will reveal them. Almost any wine is a good digestive, for it cuts grease, but this should be its least, not its only quality, even if it explains why wine drinkers are generally amiable and long lived. One of its virtues is that a bottle

Château Lafite-Rothschild in Pauillac, *has been called the Prince of Vineyards. Louis XV admired it and made it fashionable for all time and it was the favourite of Madame*

needs sharing: solitary wine drinkers are rare. The alcoholic strength of claret varies between 10°–11° which makes it far more prudent than a spirit.

The abiding factor is personal taste, but it is as well to have sufficient working knowledge of the subject to justify a personal opinion rather than a bigotry based on ignorance.

To test the truth of this the passable should always be compared with the better, glass by glass, sip against sip. If a fine wine does not show its qualities against a lesser brother, then the subject is not worth pursuing. Just as some have no ear for music or are tone deaf so the man who cannot detect such a difference must resign himself to having no palate and find his pleasures elsewhere. Fine wines are not for him: nor is this book for that matter.

Most of the best wines of the world are French, and of her two greatest vineyards the first centres round Bordeaux and the second is the long valley which has Beaune at its heart.

Claret, the wine of Bordeaux, is in name at least an English creation. The word derives from the old French *clairet* or *vin claire*, meaning a light blend of red and white wines.

Photo : Author

de Pompadour. Once the property of an English banker, Sir Samuel Scott, he sold it to the Vandenburg family who in turn sold it to the Rothschilds in 1867.

It was much favoured at Plantagenet Courts in the days of our Royal ownership of that part of France and has been popular ever since. It has been easy to transport directly by sea since the Middle Ages when a service of 300 ships was regularly employed in this traffic. Each Captain brought a fresh sprig of cypress from the banks of the Gironde to prove his authenticity.

The wine as we know it can be likened in sporting terms to a superlative amateur batsman. At his best he has no equal because of a certain apparently effortless *élan* which intensifies the spectator's pleasure for reasons beyond definition.

Burgundy on the other hand has all the virtues of a professional, it is generally more reliable and at its peak may surpass all rivals but it rarely brings that final lyric ecstasy which defies analysis or logic.

Yet the borderline between the two, except territorially speaking, is not easily identifiable. Any newcomer should hit back smartly at the superior person who sneers at the tyro who cannot detect it, for the wine snob is the enemy of the honest drinker.

The wines of St Émilion have strong affinities with those

Château D'Issan. *A fortified and moated mansion, built around 1650. Property of the Cruse family who restored it. An excellent third growth.*

grown north-west of Beaune and the minor specimens of both could be confused by better men than he.

For the beginner the simple visual guide is that claret bottles have squarer shoulders than those of Burgundy. As to taste, beyond saying that good clarets are in general more delicate, it is impossible to go. There are no words to define the flavour of a new potato to someone who has never tasted such a delicacy. Experience and experiment are the only instructors.

The newcomer too, should beware, at the start, of learned talk of years. The good vintages can of course be memorized in the same way as a schoolboy learns the dates of English kings from 1066 and most wine merchants supply a handy crib for those who wish to shine in this direction whilst still in the lower IVth. The truth is that you will rarely, if ever, see a bottle of wine in this country bearing an important name and a date which is known to be indifferent. The great Châteaux of Bordeaux do not market the wine of a poor year under their own name for they have a reputation to preserve. It is therefore sold off to those who specialize in blending and when it does appear it may be quite unrecognizable but a worthy component of something bearing a general label such as 'Superior Médoc, specially bottled for Blank and Co'.

There is nothing wrong with such amalgams, for the blender generally knows his business, which is to produce something the customer will enjoy. They are simply the lesser brethren lacking the first miracle of Cana.

The details of the merits of individual years become essential when one is buying wine for 'putting down', with an eye to the future, to long-term economy, for no wine, unless it be one that has prematurely expired or has had suspiciously rough handling, ever drops in price. It then becomes important to know that '61 for example is an exceptionally fine year and well worth acquiring with a view to having a fine cellar against the threats of 1984. It may even be very drinkable by 1970, but will surely improve.

Even so, the modern tendency is to produce a wine which will mature rapidly whenever possible and the *maître de chai*, the master of winemaking, can regulate this in the early stages and often does so.

The technique of speeding-up maturity is not mysterious or

injurious. What happens is that the grapes are *ègrapées* just after being gathered, that is, they are passed through a cylindrical device which removes the stalks and the husks which attach them to the vine itself. These last contain tannin and other vegetable acids which act as a preservative and make wines 'hard' and unpalatable in youth but ensure a sound old age. The fermentation of the wine can be further accelerated or slowed according to the time, a week to a fortnight, which the grape juice spends in an open vat before being stored in closed barrels.

All good wine merchants in Britain distinguish between wine for drinking or for cellaring and they are the best guide. Great years of the past are difficult and vastly expensive to buy, especially in restaurants. It is best to settle for a few good years still within your pocket and to decide for yourself their varying merits. If you are offered a claret from a reputable château at a price much below that of the same wine of other years the probable explanation is that it is a wine considered to be a slow maturer and not yet ready to drink, and that for some reason the vintner thinks he can use his cellar space to better advantage. In this case consult your plastic chart of vintages. You will not get a bargain to be drunk with tomorrow's dinner but an investment requiring houseroom for several years.

Mâitre du Chai. *He is the supreme authority on the practical side of wine making and cellar management.* French Government Tourist Office

A Chai at Lafite. *This is a storage room for wine in cask, at ground level. The young wine is still working, i.e. completing fermentation, awaiting the final stages, racking and bottling.*

The great wines of Bordeaux are watched from their birth by merchants who know all there is to know about vintages, whether they are buying them from their cradles, so to speak, or after they have passed through a saleroom in middle age. Thus, if you see a famous name for sale in a list at 75s 3d a bottle for a 1947 as against 25s 9d for a 1951, there are reasons for it.

Firstly, the merchant knows he can get that price; secondly the year '47 was remarkable and the wine matured quickly; and thirdly it has a rarity value. But don't buy it for tomorrow's dinner: give it a month or two to settle in its last home.

An accurate memory for a string of dates is largely a recipe for good gossip and a protection against the gentle malice of those who have taken the same 'O' levels.

Lichine, one of the greatest of authorities, says such lists are best thought of 'as a table of generalities full of exceptions'. The independent minded are quite capable of adding to their enjoyment by making their own charts from personal investigation.

Those who fancy their expertise are inclined to amuse themselves at the expense of the simple man who has a liking for wine without the mystique-jargon which sometimes goes with it. 'He fell into the simple error of confusing a Pauillac with a St Estèphe! Extraordinary ignorance.' This sort of talk is nonsense and liable to intimidate the newcomer.

Wine is for drinking and the pleasure that can be got from it is individual and not a subject for condescension. Beware of such men; they are the critics and not the public.

Only twice in my life have I seen a real expert announce correctly the name and date of a wine when it was served decanted, though I have often witnessed errors. In each case the expert did it by a slow process of deduction based on knowing his host's cellar and anticipating the trap that was being laid: the nature of the wine, that is, the information he got from his eyes, nose and palate, had only a half share in the decision.

Bracketed in importance with the wine itself is the Shipper and after him the local Merchant. Like religion, something must be taken on trust and it is wisest to put one's faith in established reputation rather than in experimenting with cut-price combines who offer goods on the 'we-can-get-it-for-you-wholesale' principle. Of course they can: what else does any merchant do? Among the big shippers to be relied on are Cruse et Fils, Frères, who own several fine châteaux. Calvet, who do their bottling in Bordeaux, Barton et Guestier, Kressman, de Luze, Lalande, Delor, Sichel, Brown Gore and Welch, and Lebègue, whose magnificent cellars are under London Bridge Station.

For the lucky few with cash and cellar space to spare a knowledge of years does become really important. Here again professional advice, always easily obtained, is probably the best, but it is undoubtedly fun to go to wine tastings and to try to pick a winner from the new growths. If you have the fortune to visit the cellars around Bordeaux you will certainly be offered clarets under three years old, far too young to drink. This is always interesting but not especially pleasing to an uninformed palate. The 'hardness' of young wines is important if they are to develop slowly and regally and few of them in youth have any agreeable

Bringing in the Vendage. *In the Médoc oxen are still used for this purpose. They are more patient than horses and petrol fumes are not good for grapes. At other times they are also used for furrowing between the vines.*

Wine Making in the eighteenth century. *The print shows every stage of gathering and pressing, including treading by foot, a practice now discontinued and forbidden in Burgundy by the Emperor Charlemagne in 809 as being unhygienic. It still obtains in Portugal.*

Cave at Mouton Rothschild. *This is the oldest part of the cellars where classic vintages are stored, often called 'The Library'. In Cognac such treasure caves are called 'Les Paradis'.*

bouquet. A new wine which shows the tyro the prospect of being really drinkable is probably one that will mature too quickly to join the company of the masters.

Tastings in England are generally organized either by merchants or societies and the sale of wine is the ultimate object. Here advice is informed and free, though it may be 'interested'.

Buying wines known to be great is like backing favourites at very short odds. The greater pleasure, with a good chance of larger reward is to spot a future winner from the field.

Wine is sometimes offered in Magnums, twice the quantity for twice the money. A good 'un in a magnum is often a shade better than its two small brothers, but by the same token the half bottle, is very slightly less satisfactory. The half bottle is more often than not a nuisance, never quite enough for two sound thinkers.

Château Beychevelle. *Built on the site of the residence of the Hereditary Grand Admiral of France, this is one of the most beautiful mansions in St Julien. The name derives from the order 'Baisses les Voiles' given by passing sailors. The story is that this was done to*

honour the noble resident, but it is more probable that the sails were dipped or struck to suit the shifting currents or the changing wind of the Gironde. *The wine is inclined to be hard in youth and slow to mature but can be among the finest in the Médoc.*

French Government Tourist Office

The Harvest reaches Home. *At Château Loudenne in the Bas Médoc the grapes are pressed in an upper room and flow into the vats at ground level. Oxen are still used. Loudenne, the property of Messrs. W. & A. Gilbey, makes red and white wines.*

A Decorative Arch *often marks the entrance to a particular vineyard. Although vines may look alike there may be a sharp difference in quality between one field and the next. This can be due to the nature of the soil but good farming plays an important part.*

The Appellation Contrôlée

On 30 July 1935, the *Appellation Contrôlée* came into force. It is the most important legislation in the history of wine for it lays down precisely the areas and *communes* which are entitled to individual names and is, in fact, a Government guarantee that the wine comes from the place stated and has not been blended with anything except a brother from the same area. This law is carefully enforced and it is rare to visit a *chai* or cellar around Bordeaux without finding an official either present or imminently expected.

Before the *Appellation Contrôlée* many lesser proprietors would dilute their products to reinforce a poor yield with something from a different district, or possibly not a Bordeaux at all. This practice is now forbidden if the words 'Appellation Contrôlée' are used on a label, but without them there is nothing to prevent a blender doing as he pleases either in France or over here.

The phrase *'Vin de la Propriété'* carries much the same weight, as does *'Mise en Bouteilles au Château Blank'* together with a date and a branded cork: these are personal and absolute declarations of content. But there are innumerable tricks to evade the letter of the law by producing phrases which look and sound almost the same. '*Mise en Bouteilles dans nos Caves*' is such a one. 'Bottled in our Cellars' of course, but just where are they? In Bordeaux or London, E.C.? *Caveat emptor*. The reputation of the Shipper and the Merchant are the true guarantees.

Appellation Contrôlées
of the Bordeaux Area

(R) = Red; (W) = White

Margaux (R)	St Julien (R)
Pauillac (R)	St Estèphe (R)
Moulis (R)	Listrac (R)
Haut Médoc (R)	Médoc (R)
Neac (R)	Pomerol (R)
Lalande de Pomerol (R)	Côtes de Canon Fronsac (R)
Côtes de Fronsac (R)	Sables St Émilion (R)
St Georges St Émilion (R)	Parsac St Émilion (R)
Lussac St Émilion (R)	Montagne St Émilion (R)
Puisseguin St Émilion (R)	St Émilion (R)

Sauternes (W)	
Ste Croix du Mont (W)	Barsac (W)
Graves Superieure (W)	Loupiac (W)
	Cerons (W)

Graves (R.W.)	
Côtes de Bordeaux St Macaire (W)	Premières Côtes de Bordeaux (R.W.)
Côtes de Bourg (R.W.)	Entre Deux Mers (W)
Sainte Foy Bordeaux (R.W.)	Graves de Vayres (R.W.)
Côtes de Blaye (W)	Premières Côtes de Blaye (R.W.)
Blaye (R.W.)	Bourg (R.W.)
Bordeaux Clairet or Rosé	Bordeaux Mousseux (R.W.)
Bordeaux (R.W.)	Bordeaux Superieur (R.W.)

The Port of Bordeaux. *This engraving shows the quayside at Bordeaux in 1730. Many of the offices, headquarters of the big* negociants *are still standing. The port does an*

Bordeaux and the Great Areas

BORDEAUX itself the second oldest port in France is a vast sprawling city, sixty miles up river from the sea, lying on either side of the Garonne just upstream from the meeting with the Dordogne where the two rivers become a wide estuary. Many of the houses of the great shippers lie alongside the quays, but the centre of the town is the Place de la Comédie and the café beneath the Grand Hotel has all the virtues of the Café de la Paix in Paris and few of its vulgarities. Opposite stands one of the finest opera houses in Europe and between them the broad street bears the main current of the city's life.

enormous trade apart from wine but the popularity of claret in England is largely due to the ease by which it can be shipped direct.

Five of the greatest vineyards in France surround the town, Médoc to the north, Graves with Sauternes and Barsac to the south, and across the river St Émilion with little Pomerol to the east of the town.

To understand these divisions the first thing to realize is that none of them is as big as an average English county. The Médoc, for example, is about forty miles long and ten miles wide at its broadest. Pomerol covers about five square miles, and Barsac only three.

The subdivisions called '*communes*' are not parishes but localities, rather in the old English sense of the word 'Hundred', related by soil or hereditary. Nor is a château of necessity a fine house; though many of them are beautiful and historic they do not compare with the great palaces around Tours. Basically they are farm houses though some of the best of them resemble the stately homes of England: but these, too, are often the centres of farming estates. The lands belonging to them are smaller than those of an average English farm. Few own more than one hundred acres of vines and some as little as five. A very rough estimate is that an acre produces a *tonneau* of wine per annum, that is to say, four barrels or 1,152 bottles, though this varies very considerably. Around St Émilion it is sometimes much larger.

Since Roman days almost every cultivable stretch of France has had vines grown experimentally upon its surface. Those that remain are the heirs of these experiments and long experience has taught perceptive drinkers where the ideal grounds lie. The total area of Bordeaux is 287,000 acres of vineyard, farmed in all by 50,000 separate growers. We are concerned only with the best of these, a few hundred which produce the finest wine on earth.

Primarily it is, of course, the soil that determines the nature of the wine; in Médoc and Graves the gravel and quartz with a sub-soil of clay and rich iron oxide; in St Émilion, the gravel and limestone. The major red grapes are the Cabernet Franc, the Cabernet Sauvignon and the Merlot. In the Sauternes area the white Sauvignon and Sémillon are in the majority, with a very small percentage of Muscadelle.

The fragrant Muscadelle grape who rarely forms more than 5 per cent of any wine, is a tricky fellow. It is he who is responsible for what is called 'maderization', that is a second fermentation which takes place in the bottle after the original process is complete. It produces a sickly musty flavour and turns the wine dark, rather like Madeira, hence the name.

The proportions used and the degree of ripeness at which they are picked are part of the art of the *maître de chai*, the vintner himself who is the arbiter of the whole process. It is the combination of the good farmer and the good farm that produces the great wine.

Visitors with an interest in the subject are welcomed in Bordeaux. The *Syndicat des Grand Vins de Bordeaux* maintains an office in the centre of the town, *La Maison du Vin*, which will give the fullest guidance to visitors and most of the chateaux will offer hospitality to strangers, being proud and delighted to show their produce. Do not expect to find the romance of wine in the *chai*, the working chamber – the best of them suggest a laboratory for producing prefabricated metagarbolized milk.

There are three or four restaurants of international reputation in the town, the best of them at the moment being Dubern, but good food is taken as logical accompaniment to wine and the problems are thoroughly understood. If you did not love wine, why should you visit Bordeaux? And if you have this most reasonable and proper interest then you are welcome as a brother, and, of course, a potential client.

The Great 1855 Classification

The wines of the Gironde were classified in 1855 by the Bordeaux brokers of the time who not unnaturally based their judgement on the prevailing price. They listed around sixty-two châteaux out of some 300 defined properties in the Médoc alone and included, very near the top, as a first growth, Haut Brion, which is in the Graves area. The Sauternes were also classified, but separately, at this date.

The St Émilions were not then highly thought of because they were cheaper though the brokers called their list 'The Great Growths of the Gironde', and they did not even rate a minor listing of their own until many years later. Snobbery and taste appear to have deteriorated and improved respectively since then.

This outdated rating has never been officially changed, though several *'Crus Exceptionnels'* have been accepted as coming immediately after the first parting and hundreds more have been added in the lesser categories. These remain courtesy titles without official authority.

A *vigneron* of the area once told me, with tears in his eyes, laughter and scorn mixed, that to expect any official change now would be impossible. There would be so much argument, jockeying and general display of Gallic temperament that the result could well be as unbalanced as the present rating. In fact as recently as 1962 the formidable *Institute National des Appellations d'Origine* itself was asked to prepare a revision but decided on reflection that it was incompetent to deal with such a delicate and tricky problem. There was wisdom if not valour in their decision.

So the old order still stands officially. It gives four châteaux or

Château Margaux. *The home of this unsurpassable wine was built in 1802 by the Marquis de Colonilla, on the side of the Château Lamothe, once the property of Edward III of England, from whom it passed in time to Baron Margaux. Amongst its many owners was the mysterious 'Marquis Conti d'Argicot', who was in reality a Monsieur Dubarry, brother-in-law of the famous royal mistress. The present owners are the Soiceté Vinicole de Château Margaux.*

The Vignoble of Château Yquem. *One of the most perfectly maintained vineyards in the world, the Yquem grapes are picked almost individually at the precise stage of 'noble decay' to make this the greatest of the Sauternes.*

crus in the first place, fifteen in the second, fourteen third, eleven fourth and eighteen fifth. After this follow the 'bourgeois' and the 'artisans'.

Even today the bigwigs of Bordeaux will raise a superior eyebrow at the praise of a fourth growth as against a second, and to admit to a liking for a 'bourgeois' is, by inference, the act of a cad. But do not be deceived by such talk: it is often the simple nonsense of traditional snobbery coupled judiciously with salesmanship. I have tasted in the Restaurant Dubern a Ch. La Tour de Mons of '47 listed as bourgeois which surpassed most of its more highly priced rivals by a distance and at Pontet Canet a bottle of their '28 which had few peers and no superiors: yet it is classed as a fifth.

The four great names in the first parting still deserve their rank. They are the Châteaux Lafite, Latour, Margaux and Haut

W. & A. Gilbey

Château Lagrange. *One of the third growths of St Julien the château was built in 1825 by Jean-Valise de Cabarrus. It now belongs to M. Andoya, and lies in a fine wooded estate, surrounded by vines.*

Brion, and to this quartet Mouton-Rothschild should undoubtedly be added, a fact which has always been recognized.

Of the St Émilion wines, Châteaux Cheval Blanc and Ausone also deserve this accolade, as does Château Pétrus in Pomerol.

An accepted usage in the trade these days is to grade wines following these masters as *Crus Exceptionnels, Grand Crus, Crus Superieurs, Crus Classé* and *Bon Crus.* The minor growths, technically *bourgeois* and *artisans* rarely display these words, disparaging to English ears, on their labels. They are often wines

34

Château Latour Carnet. *Situated in the* commune *of St Laurent, this is one of the fourth growths. The chateau produces about ten* tonneau *a year. The wine is described as 'like those of St Estèphe but with more fleshy fullness'.*

of excellent quality but not unnaturally prefer to rely on their own name, to describe themselves as *Crus Classè* and to omit the old technical rating.

The other phrase on a label which is worth noting is *Première Cuvée* which (if true) means a wine of the first pressing and is therefore the best. The words *Deuxième Cuvée* are rarely seen but they are at least a sign of honesty and this in itself is a guarantee.

* * *

NOTE: In describing the wines of Bordeaux I have outlined on the following pages a grand tour of the area starting from the northern tip of the Médoc, moving anti-clockwise to the south and so to the right bank and beyond, finishing at Blaye on the opposite bank of the Gironde. A glance at the map on page 10 will show the reader that this is a logical and simple way of making a trip which can be repeated on a dozen different routes, each with a fresh delight to offer even the most experienced wine tourist. Of course, there are omissions and they probably include somebody's darling. But not all gentlemen prefer blondes.

Drawing by the Author

Château Loudenne. *This delicate rose-pink country mansion was bought by the House of Gilbey in 1875, as proof of their status as important Bordeaux merchants. It is in the old Bas Médoc and has its own tiny port on the Gironde. The large cellars house many fine wines for export beside those grown locally.*

The Médoc

THERE are over 500 châteaux within the area, ranging from the great estates surrounding magnificent and often historic houses to small holdings of a few acres. The five important *communes* here are St Estèphe, St Julien, Pauillac, Cantenac and Margaux, and for many people these are the greatest vineyards in the world. The words 'finesse', 'body' and 'vinosity' are those generally used to describe their qualities, and the Médocs possess them all in varying degrees, though every drinker must decide between his palate and his brain where finesse ends and body begins. An entirely new set of clichés is really needed to bring the jargon back to life. But the wine's the thing, not the verbiage.

The northern third of the district was once known as 'Bas Médoc' but this prefix has been withdrawn by popular request, a concession granted curiously enough during the German occupation of France.

The wines are not particularly distinguished but good husbandry produces some which are markedly superior to that of their neighbours with the same soil. Château Loudenne, the

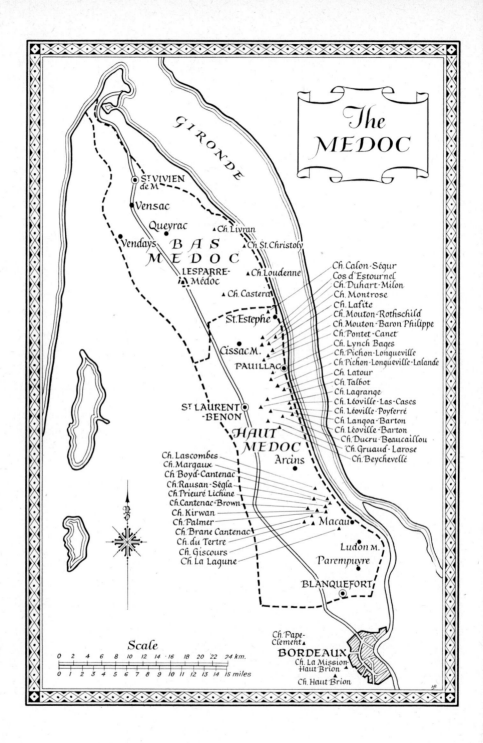

The
MEDOC

GIRONDE

Stᵗ VIVIEN de M.

Vensac

Queyrac ▲ Ch. Livran

Vendays **BAS MEDOC** Ch. St. Christoly

LESPARRE-Médoc ● Ch. Loudenne

▲ Ch. Castera

St. Estephe

Cissac M.

PAUILLAC

Stᵗ LAURENT -BENON

HAUT MEDOC

Arcins

Ch. Calon-Ségur
Cos d'Estournel
Ch. Duhart-Milon
Ch. Montrose
Ch. Lafite
Ch. Mouton-Rothschild
Ch. Mouton-Baron Philippe
Ch. Pontet-Canet
Ch. Lynch-Bages
Ch. Pichon-Longueville
Ch. Pichon-Longueville-Lalande
Ch. Latour
Ch. Talbot
Ch. Lagrange
Ch. Léoville-Las-Cases
Ch. Léoville-Poyferré
Ch. Langoa-Barton
Ch. Léoville-Barton
Ch. Ducru-Beaucaillou
Ch. Gruaud-Larose
Ch. Beychevellé

Ch. Lascombes
Ch. Margaux
Ch. Boyd-Cantenac
Ch. Rausan-Ségla
Ch. Prieuré Lichine
Ch. Cantenac-Brown
Ch. Kirwan
Ch. Palmer
Ch. Brane Cantenac
Ch. du Tertre
Ch. Giscours
Ch. La Lagune

Macau

Ludon M.

Parempuyre

BLANQUEFORT

Ch. Pape-Clement ▲

BORDEAUX

Ch. La Mission-Haut Brion ▲

Ch. Haut Brion

Scale

0 2 4 6 8 10 12 14 16 18 20 22 24 km.

0 1 2 3 4 5 6 7 8 9 10 11 12 13 14 15 miles

property of Messrs Gilbey is one of these, producing both red and white wine, but the cellars by the little private port on the estate are mainly used for the storage of other wines distributed by this enterprising firm. The Château itself, built of rose-red brick is a place of timeless charm. The names Du Castéra, Livran and Laujac are worth remembering. The latter belongs to the great Cruse empire, an enterprise with rare judgement.

St Estèphe

Moving south towards Bordeaux the *commune* of St Estèphe, at the tip of the old Haut Médoc is one of the five important districts. Here begins the area of great, incomparable wines, the aristocrats of the world. It centres around a rambling village, ancient and half alive, occasionally picturesque but always difficult and puzzling for a motorist and looks over the river from a modest height. The wines are highly individual, having an earthy bouquet suggesting flowers and fruit and rather more body than those from farther south.

The Châteaux Cos d'Estournel and Montrose are the most illustrious, closely followed by Calon-Ségur, one of the oldest vineyards in France for the title derives from the Roman 'Calones' the place name for the entire district.

Pauillac

Curiously, the name Pauillac, the next *commune*, is not nearly so widely known as, for example, St Julien but perhaps this is because the main vineyards of the district are so important in their own right. The lesser St Juliens are sound enough but completely overshadowed by their neighbours.

The little town of Pauillac is devoted to the business of wine and straggles along the river without distinction, but it possesses a substantial wooden quay or port which at high tide handles a considerable trade.

It also boasts a museum of wine which displays a dusty collection of charts and maps of interest to historians, but lacks the product itself. It is, however, the headquarters of Les Compagnons du Bontemps, a fairly recent brotherhood devoted to the admiration, degustation and sales promotion of the wines of Médoc, a worthy aim. Its members array themselves in scarlet

[continued on p. 43

The *communes* of Médoc and their Major Châteaux (Figures show the 1855 rating, plus (B) Bourgeois and (Ex) now rated *Cru Exceptionnel* and average production in *tonneaux*. One *tonneau* equals 1152 bottles).

Bas Médoc (*Now included as Médoc*)

Châteaux	Red
Castéra	39
Laujac	19
Livran	27
Loudenne	26

St Estèphe

		Red
Cos-D'Estournel	2nd	125
Montrose	2nd	100
Calon-Ségur	3rd	200
Lafon-Rochet	4th	60
Cos Labory	5th	45
Beau-Site-St-Estèphe	B	58
Meyney	B	182
Marbuzet	B	31

St Sauveur

Fontesteau	B	15
Liversan	B	96
Peyrabon	B	16

Pauillac

Châteaux		Red
Lafite	1st	180
Latour	1st	100
Mouton-Rothschild	2nd	110
Pichon-Longueville	2nd	100

The Tower of Latour *stands alone in a carpet of vines, the last relic of the original castle, being built from its ruins. It was used as a look-out against river pirates.*

Harveys of Bristol

Pichon-Longueville Lalande	2nd	125
Duhart-Milon	4th	140
Pontet-Canet	5th	200
Batailley	5th	80
Haut-Batailley	5th	60
Grand Puy Ducasse	5th	35
Grand Puy Lacoste	5th	70
Lynch Bages	5th	140
Mouton-d'Armailhacq	5th	10
Croizet-Bages	5th	50
Pédesclaux	5th	30
Clerc-Milon-Mondon	5th	50

St Julien

Châteaux		*Red*
Léoville-Lascases	2nd	170
Léoville-Poyferré	2nd	102
Léoville-Barton	2nd	70
Gruaud-Larose	2nd	185
Ducru-Beaucaillou	2nd	130
Lagrange	3rd	100
Langoa-Barton	3rd	75
St Pierre Bontemps	4th	40
St Pierre Sevaistre	4th	60
Beychevelle	4th	200
Branaire Ducru	4th	100
Talbot	4th	140
Glana	B	22
Moulin-Riche	B	19
Bontemps Dubarry	B	5

St Laurent

La Tour Carnet	4th	10
Belgrave	5th	150
Camensac	5th	40

At Château Latour *stainless steel re-*
places the old cuvés, but there is no sub-
stitute for wooden casks in which the
wine matures.

Harveys of Bristol

Cussac

Lanessan	B	38

Listrac

Grand Listrac – a Co-operative name for various Bourgeois		380

Moulis

Châteaux		Red
Chasse-Spleen	Ex	67
Robert Franquet	B	9
La Closerie Grand Poujeaux	B	23
Duplessis Hauchecome	B	34

Drawing by the Author

A Compagnon de Bontemps de Médoc. *A member of one of the twenty-three 'Brotherhoods of French Wine'. These societies exist to promote the sale and reputation of wine throughout France. The* Commanderie de Bontemps *has its headquarters at Pauillac.*

Poujeaux-Theil	B	47
Dutruch-Grand-Poujeaux	B	37
Maucaillou	B	11

Avensan

Ville-Georges	Ex	12

Soussans

Bel-Air Marquis d'Aligre	Ex	18
La Tour-de-Mons	B	65

Margaux

Margaux	1st	150
Rausan-Ségla	2nd	80
Durfort-Vivens	2nd	10
Malescot-St-Exupery	3rd	40
Ferrière	3rd	10
Desmirail	3rd	2
Marquis-de-Therme	4th	130

Cantenac

Châteaux		Red
Brane-Cantenac	2nd	125
Kirwan	3rd	60
d'Issans	2nd	12
Cantenac Brown	3rd	90
Boyd-Cantenac	3rd	30
Palmer	3rd	100
Prieuré-Lichine	4th	35
Angludet	B	27

Labarde

Giscours	3rd	90
Dauzac	5th	60
Siran	B	39

Arsac

Le Tertre	5th	100
D'Arsac	B	20

Macau

Cantemerle	5th	100

Ludon

La Lagune	3rd	65
d'Agassac	B	20

Le Taillan

du Taillan	B	10

continued from p. 39]

splendour, dine and wine superbly and trace their origins to Robin Goodfellow, the English spirit of the woods, although a 'Bontemps' is technically a wooden pail for holding egg whites used in fining the wine. Do not, by the way, translate their title as 'The Good Time Charlies': they are a very serious and high-minded body of experts.

The true glories of Pauillac are its surrounding estates which include Lafite, Latour and Mouton-Rothschild, the greatest triumvirate in the whole empire of wine.

Château Lafite-Rothschild to give its full name, belongs to the Barons de Rothschild and is a properly impressive establishment as one would expect. It truly merits the title Château and for sheer opulence it would be hard to better it. Anything less than a Rolls Royce moving through its shaven lawns to the turreted residence would, one feels, be an impertinence.

Yet the product justifies the almost insolently discreet display of splendour. It has, among other qualities, the longest expectation of life of almost any wine. Notable vintages, 1864, for example, have lasted up to seventy years in perfect condition. Every expert in the world has sung its praises and its cost matches its virtuosity, despite the very large annual yield, around 150 *tonneaux*. Enormous care is taken to ensure perfection: the grapes are sorted almost individually for imperfections and de-stalked by hand.

Mouton-Rothschild is associated, and not in name alone, with its neighbour the Château Mouton d'Armailhacq which since 1937 has been called Château Mouton Baron Philippe, for it is also a Rothschild property. Indeed the two vineyards were originally one. Rated in the old order as a 'fifth' this has now become a *'Grand Cru Classé'*.

Let me pause here to commend a very minor branch of the family, Mouton Cadet. This is a modest wine at a popular price and the contents are not specifically defined. My guess is that this is an amalgam of the poorer years, second pressings and so on. It has no claim to greatness but it is always a sound wine and on occasion is a deal better than some with more pretentious labels. My advice to the tyro is to start here: anything you find that pleases you more will be a step towards true appreciation. As a second step try the Cadet against a Pontet Canet, again listed in the old rating as a 'fifth' growth, now of course a *Grand Cru Classé*. This is always a wine of quality, rarely outstanding but utterly reliable: always in the Upper VI but never Head Boy.

There are two other *Deuxième Cru* Chateaux here; Pichon-Longueville and Pichon-Longueville-Comtesse de Lalande. The latter often provides the experts with a trick question for learners because it is now classified as a St Julien. It stands on the Pauillac borderline, a neighbour of Latour and the house itself, beautifully set among trees, is well worth seeing.

Probably no single name in the language signifies good wine as Latour, yet the estate is only 100 acres. It centres round a small rounded look-out tower built in the reign of Louis XIII out of the stones of the original castle which was sacked by the French commander Du Gueslin, when he defeated John Talbot, first Earl of Shrewsbury, in the fifteenth century and the whole area was recaptured from the English for ever. The watch tower once formed part of a chain of look-outs built to protect the countryside from river pirates and it now stands alone in as perfect a carpet of vines as one could find even in that im-

Mechanization at Latour. *A tipper truck from the vineyard deposits its load directly into the hopper, from which they are fed into the press.*
Harveys of Bristol

maculate area. Harveys the great merchants of Bristol own a large share of the property.

The wine, full-bodied and fragrant, is made from 80 per cent Cabernet-Sauvignon grapes, a very high proportion, the balance being Malbec and Cabernet Franc. Like all the masters it is apt to be hard in youth and to drink it before it reaches perfection, a minimum of fifteen years, in my opinion, is to waste good money. At its peak it is a great generous-hearted aristocrat, displaying every quality with heraldic grandeur.

There is a legend that Lord Chandos, the fleeing Seigneur of the district, buried treasure here when his castle was sacked. Despite several investigations it has never been found and I suspect that the true treasure is still where it was when Lafontaine wrote his fable on the subject.

Pontet Canet is the largest producer of the district. The Château is a large comfortable Victorian mansion, a home of the Cruse family and rightly famous for its hospitality.

Among other famous names are Duhart-Milon, Lynch Bages (always a reliable wine) Croizet-Bages, Batailley and Haut

At Château Lafite *the grapes are still moved by hand into the presses. Behind are the vats in which the wine ferments.*

French Government Tourist Office

Harveys of Bristol

Château Mouton-
Rothschild.
*Probably the
richest estate in all
the Médoc and the
producer of one of
the greatest
growths. Classed,
wrongly, as a
second in 1855, it
has always been
amongst the élite.*

Batailley. There are also innumerable small holdings who join
in a co-operative whose produce is a good example of the type
old-fashioned merchants used to call 'sound dinner wine'. These
also provide a good start for beginners or anyone with a palate
but modest means.

St Julien

The next *commune* along the Gironde is St Julien, whose
fame equals that of its neighbour. Its full title is St Julien Beychevelle and the Château Beychevelle, a graceful terraced mansion,
dominates the river at this point. It is built on the site of the
residence of the Hereditary Grand Admirals of France, in whose
honour the passing ships were compelled to dip their sails. The
name it will be seen, derives from this rule. Like all good wines
here, Beychevelle is very hard in its youth but is long lived. In

Château Talbot. *Home of one of the famous wines of St Julien. The estate has a model farm and a stud in addition to its vineyards.*

maturity it has the nature of silk velvet and a magnificent bouquet which will yield a variety of qualities to the inquiring nose or palate. Violets, syringa, strawberries, truffles, irises and wood smoke are all invoked to convey these bouquets, but they have their own indescribable individuality.

Château Talbot, the other historic name of the district is also an elegant and substantial house built on the site of the castle of Talbot, last English defender of Bordeaux, who was killed at Castillon in 1453. Again this is a fine wine and to drink it too young is to miss three-quarters of its virtue.

Curiously, these two are technically fourth growths in an area which possesses five *Deuxièmes*. They are Léoville Poyferré, Léoville Las Cases, Léoville Barton, Gruaud-Larose and Ducru-Beaucaillou. It goes to show what nonsense marches in these fine shades of classification. All these wines in maturity are superb

The Terrace at Châteaux Beychevelle *looks directly on to the Gironde. It was rebuilt in 1737 in the style of Louis XV when it belonged to the Guestier family. It was once*

The Maître du Chai of Beychevelle displaying the keys of his cellar.

Photo: Author

Photo: Author

the property of the Duc d'Epernon, Grand Admiral of France.

and at their peak could be matched but never, I think, surpassed. The output is very large and they all need at least ten and preferably twenty years before they begin to exhibit their magnificence. A man with a cellarful of these should live long and die happy.

Margaux

The fourth great *commune* of the Médoc is Margaux, dominated of course by the Château Margaux itself, which produces what has been called the King of Wines.

Maurice Healey the greatest of all authorities (because he wrote with such affectionate and limpid clarity) said of claret: 'It is *the* wine.' By this reasoning, which is hard to fault, Margaux is the wine of wines. One hundred and fifty *tonneaux* a year come from its vineyards besides a lesser wine called Pavillon Rouge and an agreeable white, Pavillon Blanc.

All the bottling is done on the spot with identifying seals and corks.

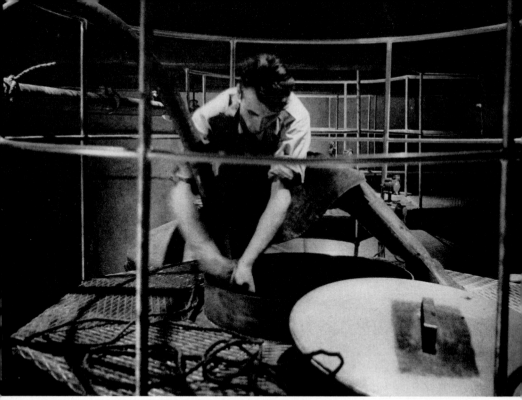

On top of a cuve *at Latour a workman connects a pipe through which the grape-juice is pumped from the press.*

The house itself lies at the end of a decorous avenue of trees, a fine Palladian mansion built in 1802 and has a suggestion of the stately English homes of old Virginia about it. Between the wars the reputation of Margaux dimmed a little among the cognoscenti but it is now, like Haut Brion, back in the absolute forefront.

Great essays have been written describing the subtleties and character of Margaux but its virtue cannot be translated to print: there is only one way to understanding and that is to drink it.

One is inclined to think of Margaux as beginning and ending with the Château itself but there are in fact four *deuxièmes*, four *troisièmes* and a *quatrième* here. They are overshadowed both in fame and in output. Château Rausan-Ségla another Cruse family possession, is the largest, producing ninety *tonneaux* against Margaux's 150, is worth noting with affection, as are Lascombes and Dufort, all of them *deuxièmes*. The Château Lascombes is the property of Alexis Lichine, one of the greatest living authorities on wine and himself the author of a masterly textbook on the subject. The house faces a decorative miniature lake and has all the elegance and grace of the ideal château of the district. The wine itself has exactly the touch of aristocracy which one would deduce from seeing its birthplace. The wines of Margaux and St Julien are reputed to mature at between seven and eight years, but the wise drinker will content himself with a minimum of ten.

Cantenac

Cantenac, the neighbouring *commune* or parish, boasts no less than eight *Crus Classés*, bearing the *appellation contrôlée* Margaux or Cantenac-Margaux. It is an area containing some of the finest mansions as well as some noble wines.

If I mention Château d'Issan first it is because of its beauty. It is a Louis XIII moated and fortified mansion, recently restored, again by the Cruse family. The wine, like the Château, had fallen upon unhappy days until the Cruse restoration but both have been returned to much of their former glory. Cantenac-Brown and Brane-Cantenac bracket themselves naturally. The former is entirely within the *commune* as is Kirwan, whereas most of the others own lands on each side of the imaginary line and now are classified as Margaux. Palmer, named by one of Louis XVIII's generals, is another of these, a typical formal mansion of the early nineteenth century. Le Prieuré-Lichine once, as its name suggests, a priory, is a century older. All these wines have a strong family resemblance which is not remarkable since the soil is gravelly and the Cabernet grape is the main supplier of the original juice.

*   *   *

Along the actual borders of the river and on the little islands there is an area of alluvial silted soil which is recent if compared with the ancient gravel. The growths here are known as Palus and the grapes are much more prolific than those from higher ground, but very inferior in quality.

Giscours in Labarde, whose records go back to 1552, is another urbanely elegant house, almost the ideal 'mind's eye' château of the area, as is Cantemerle in near-by Macau. The latter belongs to Mr Pierre Dubos one of the grand old men of the district who also owns La Tour de Mons, named from the picturesque ruin of the thirteenth-century Donjon.

Although technically a bourgeois, this can on occasion become a superb wine and were I able to speculate with a long-term cellar this would be among the first on my list.

Not far off is the Château d'Agassac, well worth a tourist visit since it is one of the most picturesque in the area, with its grey-green conical turrets and fortifications. Its wine is reasonably priced, long-lived and is again worth a modest speculation if you have confidence in judging the year.

Finally in the *commune* of Blanquefort about seven miles out of Bordeaux itself is La Dame Blanche, again a Cruse family possession. The white wine made here is dry and agreeable, but not among the great ones though in its day it has had a considerable reputation. The house and its surroundings have a lyrical beauty which are matched by its legend. The story is of an Arabian Princess who in the seventh century married the owner and became the protectress of the countryside. Her ghost, they say, still rides a white horse through the vineyards she tended and loved, and may be seen doing so (if the drifting mist permits) on any autumn morning just before the *vendange*. Horses, though not white arabs, still survive here, for there is a very successful racing stud farm attached to the long, low, white mansion.

Drawing by the Author

The Port at Pauillac. *The estuary of the Gironde is tidal and the port is still used for traffic in wine. Many of the Pauillac wines go from here upstream to Bordeaux before final shipment to world markets.*

Photo: Findlater, Mackie Todd

Château Cantemerle *in the* commune *of Macau is a fifth growth, a soft, generous wine of quality. It is a favourite wine in Holland. The history of the Château mixes fact with legend in equal proportion. Henry III of England gave it in 1242 to the Seigneur Pons de Cantemerle at a rental of two golden spurs. It had various owners under the English crown and at that time was a fortified and moated castle, with a small harbour, the centre of a feudal community. It was part of a chain of fortifications along the Gironde as a protection against pirates, mostly Danes. An elaborate communication system of pigeons and flares was used to alert the countryside. The castle also possessed a dragon who was reputed to devour enemies of the estate and traces of him can be found in the heraldic leopards of the Château. The Lords of Cantemerle and the neighbouring Château de Saugves dominated the area for centuries. The fortifications were finally destroyed in the Revolution but the Château itself has been restored and enlarged with remarkable skill. It is now the property of M. Pierre J. Dubois.*

The Comm;unes of Graves and two major Grand Crus Classé

Châteaux	Red	White
Pessac		
Haut Brion – First Growth	100	
La Mission-Haut-Brion	34	
La Tour-Haut-Brion	15	
Pape-Clément	85	
Laville-Haut-Brion		17
Léognan		
Haut-Bailly	25·5	

Châteaux	Red	White
Carbonnieux	51	68
Domaine de Chevalier	25·5	3·5
Olivier	20	85
Malartic-Lagravière	30	
Martillac		
La Tour Martillac	10	
Smith-Haut-Lafitte	42	
Cadaujac		
Bouscaut	100	50

Graves

GRAVES lies immediately south of the river Blanquefort, surrounds the town of Bordeaux itself and is about equal in area with Haut Médoc. It also encircles the two important *communes* of Barsac and Sauternes. The soil as the name indicates is gravel and despite popular belief it produces more red wines than white. This fallacy, for everyone in mentioning the word 'Graves' thinks of white wine, derives, I suppose, from the fact that Haut Brion, its most illustrious château, was placed in the great 1855 classification with the Médocs, and by nature belongs there. The official classification of Graves wines dates from 1953.

The name, they say, derives from an Irish founder, O'Brien, but the story should be bracketed with the Hibernian origin of Tim O'Shenko the Russian General of World War II. The earliest records show it as belonging to the Lords of de Brion, later called Daubrion. Pepys called it 'Ho Bryan' and drank it at the Royal Oak in Lombard Street before the Great Fire. Talleyrand who owned the château in Napoleon's time is credited with using it unstintedly to sway the fortunes of France at the Congress of Vienna. 'There never was a finer table wine,' says André Simon, speaking of its historic years, 'and no château has a more illustrious lineage or a finer wine tradition.'

Château Haut Brion *the only wine of Graves to figure in the 1855 classification is one of the five great wines of Bordeaux. Joseph de Fumel, Mayor of Bordeaux, one of its owners was guillotined during the revolution, after which it was bought by Prince Talleyrand who made great use of it at the Congress of Vienna. It is now the property of Clarence Dillon of the U.S.A.*

Château la Brède. *The moated home of the Montesquieu family produces one of the best unclassified growths of red Graves and also makes an excellent white. The white wines of this area, classified in 1959, are returning steadily to favour above their neighbours to the south.*

W. & A. Gilbey

Château La Mission-Haut-Brion *where Saint Vincent may still be seen, turned to stone, was founded by the followers of the Saint who called themselves La Congregation des Prêcheurs de la Mission. The wine, a Grand Cru Classé of Graves, ranks a little below its great neighbour Haut Brion, but well deserves its long standing reputation. Maréchal de Richelieu said of it: 'If God wished to forbid drinking why did he make wine so good?*

It fell from grace in 1922 when a new owner started experimenting with white grapes, an attempt which produced what has been described as 'just another white wine'. I do not concur with this judgement and the Haut Brion cachet makes this good wine respected in its own field.

But this epoch is over, though the white is still made with success, and the present owner, the American-born Clarence Dillon, has worked with determination to restore the true reputation. His son, Douglas Dillon, was once U.S. ambassador to Great Britain.

I drank a '45 recently and found it as near perfection as one could wish this side of Paradise, yet with a promise that old age was still a distance away. The château lies in the *commune* of Pessac, just over a mile outside the city, a noble collection of several periods that mix agreeably. Curiously, for this is rare,

Château Giscours at Labarde in Margaux is a third growth and has the proud motto: 'Primus inter pares'. Its history goes back to 1552, the first record of its sale by Gabriel Giraud, Seigneur de Labastide. At the revolution it was brought by two American bankers, John Gray and Jonathan Davis of Boston, but now belongs to M. Nicolas Tari.

there is an attractive engraving of it on the label, though the print omits the trees which surround the pile. Its neighbours La Mission-Haut-Brion and La Tour-Haut-Brion are both entitled to *Grand Cru* in the Graves Classification, which must not be confused with the 1855 edict. Laville-Haut-Brion, in the same combine, produces white Graves only. They belong to the Domaines Woltner Association and produce excellent wines in the Médoc tradition, La Mission particularly, though not in the class of Haut Brion itself. Pape-Clément is here too, a vineyard established by the Papacy when it shifted to Avignon in 1503. This might be thought a curious gesture in view of the excellent Châteauneuf du Pape from around Avignon itself. The explanation is that Clement V was originally Bertrande de Gotto, Bishop of Bordeaux. St Vincent de Paul, patron saint of Prisoners and Vintners, who died in 1660 is commemorated here by an irreverent statue, some say the saint himself turned to stone, which draws attention to the story that whilst on temporary leave from heaven (to satisfy a nostalgic thirst) he was found deeply asleep after a glorious spell in the cellars of La Mission.

Due south of Pessac lies Léognan, home of Haut-Bailly and

the Domaine du Chevalier, which with Smith-Haut-Lafitte at Martillac make the best of these noble reds.

The White Graves

At Léognan begins the white wine country which really starts at Château Carbonnieux. This dates from 1380 and like so many others was originally a Benedictine monastery. From the first it had a wide reputation, the monks even exporting their produce to Turkey where it was described as 'Mineral water of Carbonnieux' to combine religious prejudice with intelligent Sultanic taste.

In principle there are two types of white Graves, dry and sweet. They are neither of them great, which does not mean that they are not extremely drinkable, nor is there (except to the connoisseur) a very marked difference between château and château, as in Sauternes. The simple appellation 'Graves' on a bottle means that it is a blend from the area and often is all the better for it, since white wines are subject to varying vintages and a poor year's growth can be strengthened and reinforced by a better. Hence with these there is no date on the bottle and if the vintner knows his business he is improving on nature, bringing it up at least to a sound level of mediocrity. A sweet Graves is never so goldenly rich as a Sauternes and the dry is apt to be thin and lack the clean unmistakable quality of the Burgundian Pouligny-Montrachet or Chablis. All these wines mature at between two and four years.

The best that can be said for them is that they go very well with a fish when the sauce is the most important part of the dish, for then they are not quarrelsome and too strong a flavouring is apt to ruin one's appreciation of a first class wine. Château Couhins at Villenave-d'Ornon is among the best of them, and the Château de la Prade the most rewarding for tourists, a moated mansion with an historic library. By the way, a cheap bottle of Graves sometimes has an unpleasant smell of sulphur about it when first opened. This is because sulphur is, in fact, there in minute quantities having been used to remove undesirable germs or to stop the wine 'maderizing' or re-fermenting. It is not harmful and it wears off rapidly, but it does not indicate a particularly good drink. Spraying vines with sulphur is prohibited by law after 1 August each year.

Drawing by the Author

Château Yquem.

Barsac and Sauternes

THESE two important regions form a pocket beside the Garonne in the general area of Graves and are flanked on the north-west by the *commune* of Cérons and, across the river, by Loupiac and Ste Croix du Mont. The total area of Barsac is about three square miles, a quarter the size of its neighbour.

The wines are sweet (or should be) except some Filhots and go well with dessert, particularly with sharp fruits like pineapples. They are especially beloved by two completely opposite types; women with sweet teeth and experts with very learned palates. If there is a moral in this it is: never let your wife serve either wine with fish, except possibly sole Véronique. But for the best wines with fish one must go to Burgundy or to Germany.

The large sugar content is produced by picking the grapes almost one at a time, as soon as they start to rot on the vine. This state is called *pourriture noble* and is in fact caused by a fungus, *botrytis cinerea*. The same system is used with many German wines, and sometimes the process is carried much farther. Harvesting of this sort is expensive for each vine has to be culled

Château Rieussec. *A first growth of Sauternes lies on the opposite slope to Yquem and produces wholly delightful wine. After the austerities of the* chai *at Yquem, Rieussec has a*

Sauternes and Barsac: Some Major Châteaux

(Figures show average output in *tonneaux*. Classified in 1855 as First and Second Growths. All are white wines.)

Sauternes

Châteaux		
Yquem (1st Great Growth)	1st	100
Guiraud	1st	80
La Tour-Blanche	1st	25
Lafaurie-Peyraguey	1st	45
de Rayne-Vigneau	1st	75
Rabaud-Sigalas	1st	25
Rabaud-Promis	1st	35
Rieussec	1st	70
Filhot	2nd	50
Caillou	2nd	40

Barsac

Climens	1st	45
Coutet	1st	60
Doisy-Védrines	2nd	40
Myrat	2nd	40

farmhouse charm which is refreshing to the visitor. The wine is long lived and darkens with age, as does Yquem

several times and the *vendanges* have been known to go on from October to late December. The Sémillon grape when it reaches this over-ripe state has less juice than earlier and this too adds to the cost. The system gives a strong flowery bouquet. The greatest of the Sauternes is, of course, Château d'Yquem, thought by Maurice Healey to be the wine forecast by the first miracle of Cana in Galilee. It is prized above all others by the trade itself as being the true and perfect grape *in excelsis* and was rated as completely 'U' in Edwardian fiction, particularly by romantic lady novelists.

It is the longest lived of all white wines and at its best in old age, to my way of thinking, for then all the sugar has been absorbed and the resulting elixir is dark as sherry and almost dry. In its youth it is possibly for the very young who can afford to acquire expensive tastes and for vintners who already have them.

There is no bad Yquem. Nothing is allowed to leave the Château under its own label that is not up to the best and the standard is inflexible. The *maître de chai* boasts of seven 'passings' or pickings, for his harvest. New barrels of virgin wood are used for each vintage.

A 'Connetable de Guyenne' *a member of one of the more recent Orders of Wine. François Mauriac is one of the leading dignitaries.*

The house, another magnificent fortified mansion, stands on a gentle eminence looking over the vale in every direction and is an impressive showpiece built around a courtyard with a decorative well at its centre. The *chai* is austerely, almost clinically modern within and despite the two huge boarhounds who guard the place, visitors are welcome.

If you drink the proffered glass of young wine instead of expelling it professionally it will probably prove indigestible, but this advice is true of most tastings in the cellars of Bordeaux. At the time of the 1855 grading in Médoc the Sauternes were also separated into first and second growths, Yquem being declared first of firsts, in a class by itself. It has stayed that way ever since, its nearest rivals being Filhot, and to my taste, Rieussec, where the house has the appearance and quality of a well-to-do farm as it looks across the valley towards its eminent neighbour.

La-Tour-Blanche, where the undistinguished tower is in fact brown, was highly thought of by our grandfathers, but the house is now a school for young men learning to be *maîtres de chai* and the land is State controlled which may well explain its fall from grace.

The *commune* of Barsac is separated from Sauternes by the little River Ciron, a tributary of the Garonne. Here Château Climens is rated the best, indeed its wine is remarkably like an Yquem, but a trifle lighter, the difference between a Rubens and a Titian in terms of painting. Château Coutet, next door, is as near as this area comes to producing a dry wine which explains the popularity of this aristocrat.

The best of Barsac is sold either under the name of the château or simply as Haut Barsac, but the *commune* is also entitled to the appellation 'Sauternes' and the less individual half of its output appears under what is considered the more popular label.

The grapes used for these wines are 55 per cent Sémillon, 40 per cent Sauvignon and 5 per cent Muscadelle.

Entre Deux Mers

If you cross the Garonne at Cadillac you enter the country known overall as Entre Deux Mers. It lies, in fact, between the two rivers, Garonne and Dordogne and to describe them as seas is pure Gascon braggadocio. The Côtes de Bordeaux are a strip of riverside running from just above Bordeaux to Cadillac.

A great quantity of red and white wine is produced here, none of it particularly distinguished but nearly all of it acceptable. The red comes mostly from the north. Perhaps because of British indolence, which prefers a well-known name to the trouble of learning a strange one, they are not very popular over here but are mostly sold in France itself, Belgium and Germany. They have a charming bouquet and often mature early, though they sometimes improve surprisingly with age.

As might be expected their style is very like that of the wealthier Jones just across the river and this is true of the reds and the whites, though in the south the ground is higher and tougher to farm. Great reputations are achieved by making great wines consistently over the centuries. Here minor reputations rest on producing very agreeable minor wines.

The Vigneron of Bordeaux. *He is the basic farmer on whom wine depends. He is the vendangeur of October, spends his winters in deep digging and fertilizing, does the fruit pruning in November and repairs walls and fences. By February he is light ploughing with oxen and in early spring hoeing between the vines. In March he is a grafter and in April he prunes the twigs and ties up the young shoots. May finds him bedding new grafts and spraying, a task which keeps him busy most of the summer. It is his advice which generally decides the date of harvest.*

Loupiac is a little riverside *commune* entitled to its own *'Appellation contrôlée'* by the right bank, which looks across to Barsac. Its Château de Ricaud is worth noting as a very drinkable white, strongly commended with oysters or foie gras. This is where the Roman poet Ansonius had one of his villas in the fourth century. He was born in Bordeaux the son of a senator and himself became a consul. Wisely, he established his own vineyards farther north in St Émilion, which suggests that he knew a thing or two, for the ground at Loupiac is steep and gets steeper at Ste Croix du Mont, another separate *appellation* next door, so that cultivation is still almost as difficult as it was fifteen centuries ago. Ansonius was a gardener; perhaps that explains in part his move. The wines have been described as having a liqueur quality, which I translate as meaning that they have the syrupy style of a Barsac or an Yquem without their better nature.

But the majority of the white Entre Deux Mers are dry and golden and considered locally to be excellent company with the oysters of Arcachon. Neither, I think, is in a class with a Colchester native and a bottle of Chablis. On the other hand, if you are in humble mood, they go exceedingly well with Dutch cheese and will help to restore the self-respect which reflects your better nature.

Photo : Author

St Émilion. *The vines surround the town with its ancient ruins on every side. Once known as Lucaniac, every period of French history has left its mark. This is the wall of the Chapel of the Frères Prêcheurs founded by St Dominic in 1216.*

Château Montrose. *One of the two second growth chateaux of St Estèphe, the Montrose wine is distinguished by its 'earthy' bouquet and rich depth of character. It has been called 'The Model Vineyard' and 'The Latour of St Estèphe'.*

Drawing by the Author

The Tour du Roi at St Émilion *was probably built by Louis VIII. King John (Lackland) confirmed many of the privileges of the town and granted a charter in 1199 to the Jurade de St Émilion. This view from the gardens of the Hostellerie de la Plaisance also shows the ancient offices of many wine growers with the 'Vin de Côtes' vineyards behind.*

St Émilion

The Oath of the Jurade of St. Émilion

administered by the Mayor of St Émilion:—

Gentlemen, do you swear
—To defend faithfully the renown of your city and of its vine-
yards?
—To subordinate to this all your personal interest?
—To serve it by word and deed?

We swear it

Do you swear
—To safeguard the honourable traditions of your forefathers?
—To practise and show respect to your given word?
—To be united solidly in friendship?
—To exist in the pride and respect you feel for the wine of St
Émilion?
—To unite your efforts to perpetuate its glory?

We swear it

North of Entre Deux Mers on the far bank of the Dordogne lies the land of St Émilion. It adjoins the *communes* of Pomerol, Lalande-de-Pomerol, Côtes de Canon-Fronsac, Côtes de Fronsac and Neac. It is an area of intense cultivation, yielding nearly twice as much to the acre as Médoc, and has around 1,000 vineyards described as Châteaux.

Here the wines are a deeper ruby, heavier, more fruity and have a rich earthy bouquet which distinguishes them very recognizably from those of the Médoc. They are, in fact, more like the hearty giants of Burgundy. They have great delicacy at their best but it is that of a virile aristocrat not of a court beauty. The grapes are mostly a cross between the Merlot and Cabernet Franc.

The best of them come from an area about a mile square surrounding the old town of St Émilion itself, but it is nearly true to say that there is no bad St Émilion. It is always a reliable companion, the perfect associate for a steak and has the admirable quality of satisfying a robust thirst without making the drinker feel guilty of putting it to a plebeian purpose.

In fact, a simple *Appellation Contrôlée* from this district is as good a beginner's wine as one could wish and to enjoy it is to make a friend for life who will stand up in any company.

Of all the old towns and villages around Bordeaux, St Émilion is the most attractive. It stands high on the edge of the great wine-bearing plateau and bears the scars and battlements of every period of French history from the eighth century onwards. At this time the saint himself resided very uncomfortably in a cavern under a cliff, content with a rocky bed and a spring of water, which is there to this day. Young women are advised to toss a couple of hairpins into the pool: if they settle in the form of a cross they will be married within the year. The saint's disciples hewed a great gloomy monolithic church out of the rock in his memory and directly above it is the Restaurant de la Plaisance, whose gardens, food and view are the best in the whole area. Its list has every wine of the country you could wish, from the incomparable nobles to the peasantry.

Some of them have what is called the 'burnt' taste due to the grapeskins being caught by the sun and this is frowned upon by the purists though I personally find it, like any second or third

Château Bellevue in
*St Émilion is a Grand Cru
Classé, producing about
28 tonneaux of wine, a very
high yield for fifteen acres.
It is a 'Vin de Côtes' from
the higher and more stony
ground.*

The Jurade of St Émilion

Château Cheval Blanc *the leading 'vin de Graves' of St Émilion is built on the site of the inn used as a post-house by nobles travelling to Libourne to pay respects to their overlord, the English sénéschal, Roger Leybourn, who built his hunting lodge there in 1269 and created the town. It now belongs to the Fourcard-Laussac family.*

flavour a wine may offer, mightily attractive. The truth is that all the St Émilions suffer from local Bordeaux snobbery. Even to ship wine from Libourne, the little port on the Dordogne is considered *infra dig*. This may be unfair and the town still looks pretty miserable about it.

The year 1955 saw the first official classification, placing Ausone at the head of the family, above Premier Grand Cru and simple Grand Cru.

The poet consul Ansonius seems to have been the perfect aristocrat of his day, a liberal-minded lawyer, a wit, a scholar, a lyric poet of the countryside, a vintner and a lover of good living. What more could a Roman ask? Certainly he would have approved of the wine still produced in his name, for it exhibits all the qualities he displayed in life, except perhaps wit, and that can well be stimulated by a glass or two.

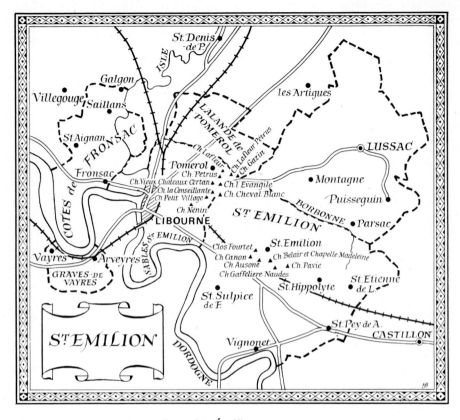

Some wines of St Émilion

First Great Growths:

	Vin de Côtes	*Tonneaux*
Ch. Ausone		14
Ch. Beauséjour-Duffau-Lagarosse		18
Ch. Beauséjour (Dr Fagouet)		30
Ch. Belair		47
Ch. Canon		75
Clos Fourtet		70
Ch. La Gaffelière-Naudes		98
Ch. Magdelaine		21
Ch. Pavie		110
Ch. Trottevieille		24

	Vin de Graves	
Ch. Cheval Blanc		84
Ch. Figeac		78

All the fine wines of St Émilion are long lived, though their span is not so great as their peers of Médoc, but they often mature earlier. The grapes are mainly Merlot and Cabernet. The second great wine of the area is Cheval Blanc. The name derives from an Inn which once stood hereabouts, up in the north-eastern corner of the *commune*. It is now an elegant almost Georgian mansion whose long-standing reputation is attributed to the varying nature of the soil which is said to change at each step. There is gravel here, limestone, silicate, and a touch of iron and this emerges in the wine itself. Of all the St Émilions, Cheval Blanc will offer the most varied delight in a single glass and this is the hallmark which distinguishes a master from a journeyman. Technically this is called a *Vin de Graves* a reference to the fact that the vineyard is on the lower more gravelly soil, whereas the majority of the great wines in the area are on the higher limestone above the town called the *Vins de Côtes*. Of these the two Châteaux Beauséjour, which differ, it seems to me, only in their proprietors, are among the best, as are Belair, which is certainly the oldest in that land, Canon, the lovely delicate Pavie, Trottevieille and the Clos Fourtet. They are all great-hearted, reliable companions.

For a typical St Émilion at a reasonable price La Tour Figeac is a fine, earthy beauty with enough strength to defy any of the heavy meat sauces.

In all there are ten Premiers Grands Crus Classées and over eighty Grands Crus among the *Vins de Côtes* and among the *Vins de Graves*, after Cheval Blanc, there are fifty-nine Grands Crus, possibly led by the Château Chauvin.

There are so many able *vignerons* here that to single one out is invidious, but I have an affection for the motto of Château Grand Barrail. *'Qui me goute, m'aime, et ne veut que moi!'* It shows a proper pride and the wine is just the stuff to convince you that it might be true: at all events it is among the princes of the *Vin de Graves*.

It must be remembered that the words 'Premiers Grands Crus Classé's do not carry the eminence with St Émilion that they do in the Médoc and in truth there is very little to choose between any of the good *Vins de Côtes*, though they can be distinguished fairly easily from the *Graves*. Apart from the masters, they are all

sound and magnificently drinkable wines but they lack the aristocracy, the delicacy of the Médoc.

At St Émilion the Jurade, the oldest of the many Orders of the area, meet. They claim with pride their origin from our own John Lackland, the luckless King of England, by a Charter of 1199 and have a certain authority to condemn wines not up to standard, but exist mainly as a sales promotion society, a duty they fulfil by frequent and splendid banquets to exhibit and consume their own products.

Château Pétrus is the leading house of Pomerol and belongs to the Loubat family who also own Château Latour-Pomerol. The wine is akin to those of Médoc but has the sap and distinction of St Émilion combined with great finesse. It is among the very best of Bordeaux and it is remarkable that its reputation, though high with experts, is not wider with the general buyer. Eighteen tonneaux a year is produced from as many acres, which is a low yield for an area generally almost over-populated with vines.

Percy Fox Ltd

Pomerol

Pomerol, the other important *commune* of the area is separated by the little River Barbonne from Lalande de Pomerol, lying directly south of it, to the north-east of St Émilion and touching the port of Libourne. The total area is under 2,000 acres, and it is dominated in every sense by the Château Pétrus, the single '*Exceptionnel*', an elegant little estate of eighteen acres.

Pomerol is often said to be more akin to Médoc than St Émilion

The Port at Blaye. *In the background are fortifications built by Vauban in 1680.*

Château Rouet. *One of the best of the Côtes de Fronsac wines is made here.*

The pumping windmill on a Château near Étauliers is a landmark on the road from Pons to Blaye.

but its wine is 'fatter' that is to say softer and more glyceriney and with more body. Pétrus in particular has an irony subsoil and this emerges very pleasantly and distinctively, giving it the 'truffle' bouquet which is greatly admired. It is an 'elegant' wine which somehow suggests rich Victorian living.

It is an area of intense cultivation, containing about fifty separate châteaux from little L'Enclos du Presbytère which produces three *tonneaux* to Nenin with its 100.

Fronsac

West of Libourne, downstream towards Bordeaux lie the districts of Fronsac and Canon Fronsac, whose wines are called Fronsadais. The *Appellation* is *Côtes de Fronsac*. Red and white are produced in about equal quantity.

The reds, which are the most agreeable of them, are honest robust fellows without much character, but good drinking, rather like the lesser Médocs.

Château Canon, which produces only ten *tonneaux*, is perhaps the most widely known of them, but the finest estate is that of Château Rouet whose wines are among the best of the area.

Bourg

Bourg, the neighbour of Fronsac on the Dordogne, makes a sound red, not unlike a St Émilion, very deeply coloured. At the Château de la Grave they produce a pleasant rosé, in addition to their reds and whites which are classed as *Grands Crus Exceptionnels*. The *Appellation* is *Côtes de Bourg*.

Blaye

The ancient and historic little port of Blaye is the focal point of the last large area of vineyards. It looks across the wide Gironde towards the heart of the Médoc. It was the headquarters of the young Louis XIII when his troops attacked and captured Bordeaux and is the reputed burial ground of the valiant knight Roland and his wife Aude. He was killed at Roncevaux but the site of his basilica is obliterated by an ugly fortress.

A very great quantity of red and white is produced here but in the main it is insipid stuff of no outstanding character and it is mostly used for blending.

At Plassac there is the Château Bellevue, remarkable for its grotesque baroque Victorian Gothic architecture, which rates an area *1ere Cru Exceptionnel* but would not, I think, do so in the face of great competition.

The grapes of the district are Malbec, Cabernet and Merlot.

A wine basket, though useful for serving, should not be used with Château-bottled wines. The ideal claret glass is by Baccarat.

Serving Claret

WINE should always be stored on its side until the last days of its life. Wine shops displaying their goods upright, should be avoided and no reputable merchant would think of doing so. The ideal cellar temperature for reds is 52°F but the most important factor is that it should not vary.

The day before drinking (some say two) the bottle should be stood up in the room in which it is to be drunk, and allowed to warm gently to its surroundings. The case of white wines is quite different: an hour in a refrigerator will improve them more efficiently though less decoratively than a bucket of ice.

The cork of a youngish wine, up to ten years, can be drawn an hour or possibly two, before drinking, but even this rule is subject to individual theories. Many authorities give fifteen minutes as the upper limit. What is certain is that the older the bottle the shorter must be the interval between uncorking and drinking. A *very* old wine sometimes lives only a few minutes after uncorking.

A great deal of fuss is made about the business of a wine being 'corked', that is, having a cork which has gone bad and so infected the contents of the bottle, to its utter ruin. The truth is that no one with a sense of smell can miss a corked bottle: it has the stale reek of decay.

Many wine waiters, if accused by a client who wishes to shine as an expert, will agree that a bottle is wrong and rush off for another, but the real answer is very likely to appear on the bill in one form or another.

The neck of the bottle should be wiped clean both inside and out because any dirt or scrap of metal from the capsule may easily ruin the flavour.

If the wine is to be decanted this should be done with infinite care and very slowly.

This practice is beloved of wine waiters, who often 'win' themselves a drink in the process. The important thing is to make sure that the decanter is absolutely clean and that the wine is not

Two wine funnels. The one on the left is Victorian and the other George III has a filter and the correct curve to direct the wine to the side of the decanter.

For decanted wine the carafe on the left of the bottle is the best of the modern shapes and lighter to handle.

jostled on its way. Many antique silver shops still sell funnels for this purpose and they are not only decorative things but fun to use. The best of them have a curve at the narrow end so that the wine strikes the side of the decanter first and does not drop directly to the bottom. There is another advantage to decanting; a good wine looks superb in cut glass on any table.

Basket cradles, again a restaurant fetish, produce violent arguments on both sides, one school holding that it is an easy and gentle way of handling a fine wine and the other that once a bottle has been stood upright it should remain that way until it is poured and that a cradle causes any sediment to mix again. I am bound to say I side with the latter. No Château bottled wine should be treated like this. An ordinary fellow bottled from a cask by your wine merchant is unlikely to throw a sediment and in this case a basket makes for ease of serving.

Once in a glass, a wine is often improved by twirling it around, which brings out the best of its qualities at the right moment. For this reason a wine glass should never be more than two-thirds full. If your palate tells you the wine is too chilly, allow it to breathe a little before drinking and hold the glass in the palm of your hand to let it warm.

The second glass of a good wine, unless it is of great age, is almost invariably better than the first, partly because of this 'breathing' and partly because your own palate is by then free of any *arrière-pensée* caused by its predecessors.

These are the finer points of wine butling. An ordinary claret of unknown lineage is almost invariably improved by being drunk a mite above what is called 'room temperature'and though it will be fatal to your reputation as a connoisseur if you are caught at it, a dunking in warm water, in an emergency is better than serving a cheap wine stone cold. A far better method is to decant a simple wine into a warm carafe. A hot cupboard may also be called into service.

The best of corkscrews is possibly the double screw made largely of boxwood, because this does not jog the wine in the process. If a cork breaks and becomes an infernal crumbling nuisance, always decant through a filter. If your splendid silver funnel does not have a strainer incorporated, a fine mesh tea-strainer will do the job just as well.

Finally, remember that wine is a living thing and needs delicate handling at all times. If you suspect that a purchase has had several recent changes of hands before it reaches you, give it ample time, a month at least, to settle down.

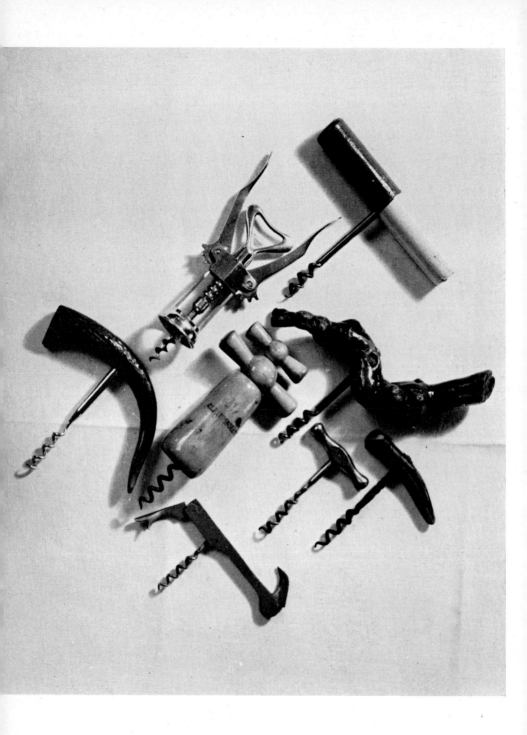

Vintage Claret

(*Note:* All charts are generalities. Your wine merchant should know if a wine of a great year is now reaching its peak and should be drunk now (1947, for example) or if the wine has a long expectation of life.)

Year	Red	White
1961	Very good	Very good
1960	Average – thin. Quick to mature	Average – thin
1959	Very good, full of body	Excellent
1958	Fair. Light	Good 'Elegant'
1957	Good all round. Small	Excellent. Great bouquet
1956	Average. Small yield from frost	Average. Small yield from frost
1955	Excellent. Delicate	Excellent. Delicate
1954	Fair. Light	Fair. Light
1953	Great. Stylish – heavy	Great. Delicate
1952	Very good. Light	Good – delicate
1951	Poor but a few good	Mediocre
1950	Good – elegant	Mediocre
1949	Very good. Full	Very good. Full
1948	Very good. Robust	Good. Bouquet
1947	Great. Rapid maturers	Great. Sweet
1946	Fair. Elegant	Mediocre
1945	Excellent. Strong and slow to mature	Excellent. Rich
1944	Average. Light	Mediocre
1943	Very good	Great
1942	Good. Full	Very good – sweet
1941	Mediocre. Thin	Mediocre

Classic Years

1937	Great but matured rapidly
1929	Full-bodied. Still improving
1928	Very graceful. Some only just ready
1926	Fine but very little left. Developed quickly
1924	Full, fine bouquet
1921	Elegant
1920	Good all round

Some French Wine Terms

Amertume and *Astringent*	Sharpness or bitterness, caused either by youth or travel from which the wine has not yet recovered, or again it may be due to a poor harvest and unripened grapes.
Bouche	Mouth. A Vin de Bouche is traditionally 'top table' i.e. the best.
Bouquet	The scent of a wine. This should be discreet, pleasing and varied, i.e. reminiscent of more than one flower or fruit.
Chai	A preparation or storage room for wine in cask as against a cellar, which is below ground
Bouchonné	Corked. A bottle ruined by a rotting cork.
Cave *Caveau*	A cellar.
Chambrer	To bring a wine to room temperature. In England this should be over rather than under done.
Complet	Complete. A high compliment: only the best wines and years qualify for it.
Corsé	Robust. Either having a high alcohol content or giving the impression of plenty of body.
Coupé	Blended with another wine, technically 'cut'.
Cuve	Vat. 'Tête de Cuvée', the first selection of the best and 'Première Cuvée', the best of the wine from one pressing.
Finesse	An aristocratic taste, a delicacy pleasing to the palate.
Goût	Taste.
Goût de Terroir	An earthy taste, suggesting the soil of the particular vineyard.
Madérisé	A wine that has become sweet owing to a second, unwelcome, fermentation. Tasting like a Madeira.
Moelleux	Soft. Luscious, flowing roundly over the palate.
Mou	Flabby.
Mouillé	Watered.
Mûr	Ripe.
Negociant	A middleman who buys from the Château and re-sells either locally or for export.

Pourriture Noble	The mould or rot on a grape which increases the sugar content in Sauternes, etc.
Soyeux	Silky. Smooth, without the harshness caused by tannin.
Soutirage	Racking. The cleaning or refining of wine with the addition of whites of eggs which collect the suspended impurities.
Tendre	Tender, gently pleasing, but inferring possibly a short life.
Tirage	Bottling.
Tirage d'Origine	Original bottling at the place of origin, generally with stamped corks.
Velours	Velvety, in the sense of soft and full.
Vendange	The grape harvest.
Vigneron	A vine grower or a worker in the vineyards.

& Cº 2280

LONDON

L'ENVOI

L'Envoi

EVERY book on wines has its errors, some of fact, some of opinion. The output of the vineyards, for example, varies from year to year and it is difficult to make an average. What one palate finds 'earthy' another will find 'coarse' and a third 'full blooded'.

But wines are above all, friends, companions worth cultivating in all their moods and all their social classes and therefore worth respecting and discussing familiarly. Some, of course, are always welcome; others must be offered house room on particular occasions or for particular reasons.

Beware then of the man who runs down your family circle or pretends to an intimate acquaintance with the aristocracy for the sake of name-dropping. One of the virtues of wine is that having settled your affection it will remain faithful and given the chance will improve with longer acquaintance.

The happiest man is he who has a wide circle of such friends and can gossip about them without condescension. Such a one was Maurice Healy whose *Stay Me with Flagons* is the best book ever written about wine since it contains no statistics or charts but is a tapestry of gracious memories of matters which gave a lifetime of innocent but cultured pleasure.

I wish you all good drinking and may you never lack a companion for your companion.

Some Books on French Wine

MAURICE HEALY, Stay me with Flagons

LOUIS JACQUELIN and RENÉ POULAIN, The Wines and Vineyards of France

P. MORTON SHAND, A Book of French Wines

ANDRÉ SIMON, The Noble Grapes and the Great Wines of France

DENIS MORRIS, The French Vineyards

ALEC WAUGH, In Praise of Wine

J. R. ROGER, The Wines of Bordeaux

RAYMOND POSTGATE, The Home Wine Cellar

RAYMOND POSTGATE, The Plain Man's Guide to Wine

ALEXIS LICHINE, Wines of France

C. W. BERRY, In Search of Wine

H. WARNER ALLEN, The Contemplation of Wine

H. WARNER ALLEN, Through the Wine Glass

T. E. CARLING, Wine Aristrocracy

ANDRÉ SIMON, A Wine Primer

*   *   *

LOUIS CRIZET, Les Vins de France

LOUIS CRIZET, Le Vin

Le Vin de France dans L'Histoire

LA SOCIETÉ DE L'ANNULAIRE DE LA GIRONDE, Les Grands Vins de Bordeaux

HENRY RIBADIEU, Les Châteaux de la Gironde

YVES RENOUIL and PAUL DE TRAVERSAY, Dictionnaire du Vin

L. LARMAT, Les Vins de Bordeaux

*   *   *

JACQUES SCHMITT, Die Wein Frankreichs

ACKNOWLEDGEMENTS

I am extremely grateful to the French Government Tourist Office, Mr E. L. De Rouet of Brown, Gore & Welch, Mr Guy Prince of Lebègue, Mr Harry Waugh of Harveys of Bristol, Mr W. L. Binns of Findlater, Mackie Todd, Mr 'Tubby' Ionides of Percy Fox Ltd, W. & A. Gilbey, Mr John Wheeler of Lay & Wheeler, and Mr John Hortin, the most distinguished amateur I know, all of whom in many and various ways have helped with all that is best in this book.